S

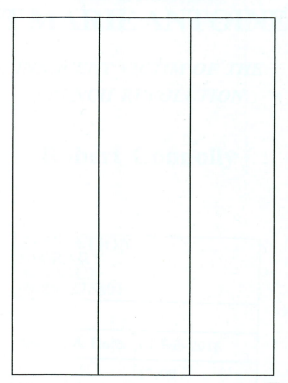

ARTHUR H. STOCKWELL LTD
Torrs Park   Ilfracombe   Devon
Established 1898
www.ahstockwell.co.uk

British Library Cataloguing-in-Publication Data.
A catalogue record for this book is available
from the British Library.

Arthur H. Stockwell Ltd bears no responsibility
for the accuracy of events recorded in this book.

ISBN 978-0-7223-3960-2
Printed in Great Britain by
Arthur H. Stockwell Ltd
Torrs Park   Ilfracombe
Devon

SAINT MARIE ANTOINETTE
Innocent Victim of the French Revolution

On 14 July 1789, the Bastille, hated prison and symbol of oppression, was stormed by Parisian revolutionaries and razed to the ground. With this violent act the French Revolution exploded into reality. Events gathered momentum during the autumn of the same year, and a revolutionary mob marched to Versailles Palace on the evening of 6 October to demand the removal of the royal family to Paris. The popularity of the royal family had been in continuous decline, and the Queen, Marie Antoinette, was disrespectfully referred to as 'The Austrian', being singled out unfairly as the malign guiding force behind all the unacceptable attitudes and decisions of her husband, the incompetent King Louis XVI. The King and Queen were left with no other choice but to bow to the demand of the revolutionaries, who escorted them, their children and entourage back to Paris. They were installed in the Tuileries Palace, which had been the royal residence prior to the construction of Versailles Palace.

The family's incarceration in the Tuileries Palace severely restricted their lifestyle, enabling the revolutionary leaders to keep a close watch on the royals and their associates, with spies in every category of employment.

For twenty frustrating months they lived in the old palace under the ever watchful eyes of numerous revolutionary guards, continuously urged by friends to escape from France whilst they still had the chance. At last the King and Queen, in collusion with the Queen's besotted Swedish admirer, Count Fersen, formulated a plan of escape to Belgium.

Everything was arranged for the night of 20 June 1791. Count Fersen had secured false documents for all members of the party. At the appointed hour the royal family and friends, each in their various disguises, were safely assembled in a berlin, also acquired by the Count.

Count Fersen played a leading role in the first stage of the flight from the Tuileries Palace. He sat next to the coach driver and directed the latter along the pre-planned route non-stop to Bondy, a suburb of Paris, which they reached an hour later. At that point the King decided not to subject the Count to any further risk. There were two coaches and several other loyal helpers willing to take their chances on behalf of the royal family; so after a brief discussion and fervent farewells the Count rode off into the darkness towards Paris, having arranged to rendezvous with the royals in Austria.

Thereafter the slow progress and unconcerned attitude of the royal party enabled word of their escape to be carried on ahead of them and resulted in their flight being brought to an abrupt end in the little town of Varennes in the evening of 21 June, as the sun was setting in the western sky. The town of Montmédy, where they would have been safe, was a mere thirty miles distant.

The King and Queen, their son and daughter, the King's sister (Madame Elizabeth) and the children's governess (Madame de Tourzel) were lodged overnight in the Bras d'Or Hotel in Varennes, where they were well treated, even though they were under close arrest. The only road into and out of the town was barricaded on a bridge under which flowed the river Aire.

Their flight had ended.

The following morning, 22 June 1791, after a much needed rest, the royal party boarded the berlin for their return journey to Paris under heavy guard.

During a quiet, pensive moment, Marie Antoinette reflected privately on their plight:

VARENNES

Farewell, Varennes,
Pretty little town where joy and sorrow unexpectedly met,
When fate callously sprung its trap
And delivered us back into the hands of our enemies,
As the all-embracing sun its glowing embers set.
O, how devastating! All lost in a moment of recognition,
When safety was so near and yet so far away
And stifled was its expected cheer.
And now our slow return to Paris, paraded in disgrace,
Whilst the future hides its face in fear.
But, do not be sad, Varennes, little town on the Aire.
You were the innocent setting that welcomed our intrusion.
The vagaries of fate decide the route that we must take,
Whether success or failure waits to greet us at its conclusion.

Farewell, Varennes.
Perhaps we will meet again one future day
When spring is in radiant bloom.
And farewell to your pretty little river,
On whose furrowed brows I spill my sad sighs.
And so alas! we part, but not for ever, I pray.
Adieu, adieu, Varennes.

* * * * *

The unsuccessful escape attempt brought in its wake demonstrations of hatred and vile abuse, with the Queen again being unfairly singled out as the unfortunate scapegoat.

Security at the Tuileries Palace, after the return of the royal family, was enforced to such a degree that it made escape virtually impossible. Guards were even posted in the King and Queen's bedrooms, where only a screen separated the prisoners from the officers guarding them.

When Count Fersen heard of the Varennes interception he was shocked, and, the following year, after receiving a secretly delivered letter from Marie Antoinette, he returned to Paris disguised as a courtier. The outlook for the monarchy was steadily worsening.

Count Fersen gained an audience with the King and Queen and proposed another escape attempt. The King declined the offer, deciding instead to face whatever fate had in store for him. That same evening the Count wished the King and Queen a successful conclusion to their present predicament, voiced his farewells to them and departed. They were never to meet again.

The revolutionary unrest continued through the sojourn of the royal family in the Tuileries Palace and came to a climax on 10 August 1792, when the palace was stormed and the Swiss guards were massacred. The royals had previously been forced to take refuge in the National Assembly, and a few days after the event (on the 13th) they were imprisoned in the Tower of the Temple Palace in Paris. Here, supervision was intensified. The family's meals were closely examined and a guard was always present in their living quarters as well as in their bedrooms. Security was designed so as to leave nothing to chance.

Gradually the King and Queen, their daughter Madame Royale, their son the Dauphin and the King's sister, Madame Elizabeth, settled into their cramped surroundings and developed a daily routine. The governess, Madame de Tourzel, had already been removed.

The King took charge of his son's lessons whilst the Queen and Madame Elizabeth instructed the daughter. The family was allowed to take supervised walks in the palace gardens, but Marie Antoinette, humiliated and deeply hurt by the mocking, abusive language of the uncouth revolutionary guards, often remained in the apartment and busied herself by reading and sewing. Sometimes she reminisced, juggling the past with the present and the unknown future:

JOY AND SORROW

O, what joy to live again the childhood innocence of sweet content!
In the corridors, rooms and gardens of Schönbrunn Palace,
Where life was a daily carousel, a joyous event
And gratitude to God was expressed
Thru' hymns in the Latin Mass.
I remember well the times when little Mozart came,
Barely a year younger than I.
We sang and played together in the corridors and gardens,
Unaware of future fame,
And the only fleeting moment of regret was the parting goodbye.
And sisters and brothers too,
All cherished jewels in my childhood years,
And now dispersed across Europe
In impressive castles and royal dress,
Whilst I, a rejected queen, with my loved ones,
Languish in this Temple Tower, haunted by gnawing fears.
And the spirit of hope in subdued voice fails to impress.
What uncertain future awaits us now?
Will the fleur-de-lys bloom again to breathe its joy?
Or will it fall beneath the onslaught of the revolutionary plough
And for evermore among the history pages lie?
I, Marie Antoinette, am now a pawn of circumstances,
A scapegoat for the most vile, ambitious men with an insatiable thirst for power,
And yet I would willingly forfeit my life for the assurance of my loved ones' survival chances
And in death face my judgement above,
After I had said farewell to freedom in that final moment of my fatal hour.
Amen.

* * * * *

Shortly after their removal to the Tower the unhappy Queen was sitting by the bed where her young son of seven years of age had fallen asleep. His sweet innocence evoked the memory of a five-year-old black African boy (by this time he would have been nine years old), who had been brought to Versailles from his native home by a sea-faring merchant as an object of amusement for the King. The Queen had been far from amused. She had unleashed her anger on the surprised merchant and scolded him for his lack of Christian values in taking such a young child from his natural parents. She had reminded the merchant and others present, including the King, that the unfortunate child, now an orphan, was deserving of the same respect and loving care, regardless of colour, as every other child of God. She thereafter, with the King's support, had the little boy baptised in the Catholic faith with the names Jean Amiliar Muller, and she placed him in the care of an older palace boy. He was educated and given the loving care he needed – and much of that was from the Queen herself.

After the royal family's removal from Versailles, the compassionate Queen didn't forget the little African boy. She had him placed in a residential boys' home and she funded his welfare and education. Now imprisoned in the Tower and deprived of all sources of income, she was powerless to help him and could only sadly visualise his innocent face whilst expressing her anxiety and hope for his present and future state:

THE ORPHAN BOY

Dear Jean Amiliar Muller,
Deprived orphan of misfortune,
How fare you now in this fearful hour,
Without the sous to ease your plight?
Not wandering alone I pray,
Thru' the dangerous streets of Paris,
Whilst I, imprisoned in the Tower
And out of reach,
Can only pray thru' anguished day and night
That you are alive and well in some safe haven
And that God in loving watch will guide you if in wandering
  flight.
Farewell, poor child of misfortune.

* * * * *

Marie Antoinette's concern for the little African boy carried her back to her early years as queen, when she had rescued another young boy. Armand, accompanied by his grandmother, had been begging from the occupants of passing carriages. The Queen, on noticing the pair, had her carriage brought to a standstill. She was so moved with compassion by the plight of the woman and her pretty four-year-old orphan grandson that she not only emptied her purse and gave its contents to the woman, who she learned had several other orphaned grandchildren to support as well, but she also offered to adopt the innocent child and have him brought up and educated at Versailles. The grateful grandmother was granted whatever time she needed to think about the generous offer of the graciously condescending Queen. Contact details were exchanged and a little later the grandmother, full of joy and sadness for the advantage to and loss of her grandson, reluctantly agreed to the Queen's proposal. Sometime later Marie Antoinette had also adopted Armand's six-year-old brother and, in addition, granted a personal allowance to the grandmother. The allowance was paid at regular intervals, for herself, her husband and the rest of her orphaned grandchildren. The Queen had played a leading role in the welfare and education of the two boys, until the birth of her own first child. Thereafter she paid for the boys' studies and retained a personal interest in their education.

They were now young men aged sixteen and eighteen. The eldest had become interested in music and, as far as the Queen knew, he was still involved in that field of study, but she wondered what had become of little Armand:

ARMAND

O, my dear Armand,
From the austere byway to the bosom of my heart,
And now you wander I know not where.
But I pray that you are safe
In these uncertain days of turmoil and death.
Has the revolution roused your loyal roots
And tempted you to play a part?
If so, I cannot condemn, but wish you well
And pray that you do not dare speak openly of me with affection.
But in your prayers remember the angel of mercy,
Marie Antoinette.
Farewell, my dear little orphan boy.

* * * * *

On 11 December 1792, the royal family suffered another setback. The King was, without warning, removed from the family group and placed in another apartment lower down the Tower. He didn't see his family again for almost six weeks. Just prior to his removal his private papers had been discovered in a secret drawer in the Tuileries Palace, and they were, during his following trial, to prove instrumental in his conviction. The subsequent death sentence for high treason, which was announced on 20 January 1793, was carried out within twenty-four hours.

The King was reunited with his family on the eve of his execution. The reunion was heart-rending, with unleashed sorrow, lamentations and endless tears. The emotional meeting lasted two hours and ended with the King lovingly embracing each heartbroken member of his family. Marie Antoinette could only be comforted by the promise of a meeting with her condemned husband the following morning before he departed for La Place de la Revolution, where he was to be executed under the blade of the guillotine. The King knew he would not keep his promise; he couldn't bear to subject his grieving family to the trauma of another parting.

On the morning of his execution he participated in the offering of Mass in his apartment before quietly leaving for his fatal appointment.

Marie Antoinette had lain awake most of the night, weeping and praying for a miracle to happen. At daybreak she prepared herself for the final meeting and waited patiently, believing that the longer she waited the better his chances of avoiding the guillotine. However, all her hopes were ended when suddenly the drums of death rolled out their chilling message, followed by the revolutionary cries of "Vive la republique!" and "Vive la liberté!" She clasped her son and daughter and Madame Elizabeth, and the inconsolable group sobbed for hours.

That same night as she lay awake in bed in the seclusion of darkness and with tear-stained eyes, engulfed by sadness, she felt the guilt of the King's tragic demise. She could see his image vividly in her mind and, whispering almost silently because of the ever present guard a few metres distant, she confessed before falling asleep from sheer exhaustion:

CONFESSION

O, my beloved Louis,
Your memory lingers on my every thought
And its presence caresses my sorrowed heart,
As I stoke the embers of guilt
That illuminate the sins of my inadequate past,
Which, by unseen design and slow degrees,
Marked your tragic end from the very start.
Now, your grieving widow,
I mourn your loss and that of your devoted love,
Whilst I ponder deep
Where the safety of our loved ones lies.
And I pray that my alleged sins will not also be instrumental
In extinguishing life's pulsating glow from their innocent eyes,
But I fear to think beyond this moment now.
Amen.

* * * * *

The days and weeks following the execution of Louis XVI were clouded in a mournful atmosphere affecting all members of his family. The restrictions of their imprisonment left precious little to divert their attention. Watching eyes and alert ears noted everything that was done and said.

Marie Antoinette's nagging concern was for the safety and well-being of her two children, whom she dearly loved. She was prepared to forfeit her life for them at any time, in return for guarantees of their freedom and future survival. Often as they sat quietly reading their books she would watch and mentally repeat her wish:

THE WISH

O, my cherished loved ones,
So angelic in thought,
So innocent in life.
If I were but to know,
Beyond the whisperings of doubt,
That your obscure future was to be in safe surroundings spent,
I would within, in loudest voice, my grateful thanks to heaven
*   shout,*
And, without anguish or complaint,
Summon all my strength and devote my ill-measured time to
*   prayer*
And face my end with dignity, content.

* * * * *

The compassionate Queen was not without friends. On two occasions during the spring and summer of 1793, plans to rescue her and her children were formulated, but each time they had to be aborted late on. It was as though fate was against them.

More heartbreak was to follow that of the King's execution. Late on the night of 3 July 1793, officials of the Revolutionary Commune arrived at the Tower with orders for the Queen's eight-year-old son, the Dauphin, to be transferred to the apartment that had been occupied by the King prior to his death. The sleepy-eyed boy, terrified and with his eyes awash with tears, threw himself into his mother's arms and begged to stay. The shocked and heartbroken mother, Marie Antoinette, weeping and overcome with emotion begged for compassion and consideration – but to no avail. She was left with no alternative but to accept the order. She made a great effort to compose herself for her son's sake and, together with her daughter and Madame Elizabeth, she succeeded in calming her young son as they prepared him for his departure. He then tearfully embraced each of them in turn and made his heartbreaking, reluctant farewells. His mother showered him with affectionate kisses and reassuring words whilst dampening his hair with her sorrowful tears. Then she watched as he departed, still crying, with the officials, not knowing if they would ever meet again.

Later that same night, as she lay grief-stricken on her bed, in the seclusion of darkness, shedding endless tears, she silently lamented the brutal abduction of her beloved son:

THE LOSS OF HER SON

O, my beloved son,
Stolen from your distraught, heartbroken mother
And now languishing all alone in fearful loneliness below,
So near and yet so far away.
Do not be afraid, my precious little one,
For you are in my every thought and supplication to God, that
    continuously grow,
To comfort and console you and wrap you in his loving caress.
And I invoke the spirit of your loving, departed father to watch
    over you
Thru' these depressing days of haunting distress.
O, how utterly cruel the immoral mentalities of ambitious men,
To subject an innocent child to the mental torture of solitary
    confinement
And his grieving mother to the depths of despair,
Where suicidal whisperings infiltrate to harass and torment!
But I must be strong, and I must believe beyond all self-care,
That both you, my son, and your sister –
My beloved children –
Will survive the anarchy that spreads in wild confusion,
Even if it has to be at the expense of the ultimate sacrifice:
My execution beneath the hated guillotine,
Where all life's pulsating aspirations are severed to satisfy
    solution.
Do not be afraid, my little one, for I am not far away,
And your loving sister lies sleeping close-by, exhausted by
    sorrow,
But I will continue to pray for you thru' the darkness of night,
And I pray too that the flower of hope will bloom again
    tomorrow.
Amen.

* * * * *

During the days following her son's departure, Marie Antoinette spent hours on end watching from a small window, hoping to see him momentarily as he walked to the Tuileries gardens accompanied by his tutor, the illiterate cobbler, Simon. The forced separation deeply affected the distraught Queen, both physically and mentally, just as her captors meant it to. Knowing that he was lodged in the apartment below, and that she was able, at times, to catch sight of him in passing, brought a little comfort to her troubled state.

On 1 August 1793, it was whispered to her that she was about to be moved from the Tower to the Conciergerie. Aware that she was about to be parted from her daughter and Madame Elizabeth so soon after the loss of her son, and feeling that she might never see any of them again, added heavily to her grief. The ordeal of the previous two years showed on her still pretty, but ageing, face. Her hair had already begun to turn grey and her health was deteriorating. She looked much older than her thirty-eight years. That same evening, as she lay in bed in the darkness with tears cascading down her harrowed face, she addressed herself in thought to her beloved children:

THE AGONY

Sleep, my precious loved ones
Both here and below.
Sleep well.
My only crumb of comfort is that you cannot see the starting
Of my unbridled anguish within,

Nor hear my weeping,
As I suffer now the agony of our parting.
To the Conciergerie, the abode of the condemned,
I am compelled to go,
By those cruel, unyielding forces that ravage France.
And there, alone within the confines of a lonely cell,
I must, as your noble father did, with pious ambition,
Prepare myself to advance
And meet my conspired end.
Do not fret, my loved ones,
For you will always be close to my heart
And even in death,
After the cold blade has bathed itself in my blood,
We shall not be far apart.
Farewell, my precious jewels;
My heartbreak is a Gordian knot that can only be undone by
*   the guillotine blade*
And therewith I pray my misery and yours will be ended,
And my debt to France duly paid.
Until we meet again, my beloved children, in heavenly embrace,
*   farewell.*

* * * * *

Later that same night her sorrow was interrupted by the arrival of officials and revolutionary soldiers. She was duly informed of her immediate transfer to the Conciergerie, then a prison in the Palais de Justice, which was also the headquarters of the Revolutionary Court. Here enemies of the state were tried and sentenced, and it was here that Marie Antoinette would later appear before the tribunal. With the help of her daughter and Madame Elizabeth, who were also suffering, she hastily dressed and made a parcel of clothes. Then, after affectionate, tearful embraces and emotional farewells, she quickly departed with her escort. As she passed the door of the apartment where her young son was lodged below, she felt the urge to call out to him, but she managed with great effort to stifle the strong motherly instinct. She realised that it would only add to his grief if he were to guess the truth.

At the Conciergerie, the jailer, his wife and her assistant, a young illiterate girl, Rosalie Lamorliere, who did as much as she dared to make life bearable for the deposed Queen, were waiting to receive her. She was entered in the register as Madame Marie Capet (Capet was the dead King's surname), prisoner number 280, a conspirator against the Republic of France.

Her cell, a mere four by four metres, was divided by a screen so as to give her a little privacy from the eyes of her two guards. The cell was impregnated with damp, which helped to worsen the ill-health of the prematurely ageing Queen. Her pathetic existence, and the uncomplaining and dignified manner in which she accepted it, softened the hearts of her guards; and one of them was so moved that he sometimes brought flowers for the gentle, grateful Queen.

A couple of weeks after arriving at the Conciergerie the revolutionary administrators confiscated one of her prized possessions – a little gold watch that she had brought with her from Vienna twenty-three years before. She was quite upset about its loss and, that night in the privacy of the dark night, she tearfully lamented and silently reminisced on her youth:

MEMORIES

O, joyful youth,
So carefree, so unaware,
So bold, so true,
So admired, so envied,
Like a radiant rose in fragrant bloom –
Life's unblemished jewel indeed!
Such was I, and such was my tiny gold watch.
But as I aged and lost my flush of youth,
My fragmenter of passing time, my little treasure,
Kept its ageless beauty.
And now alas! we too are separated
And I mourn with tears the loss of my only pleasure.
Light and dark are my silent companions now,
And O, how I miss you, youth,
And my tiny gold watch – my time sage,
Whose nostalgic voice I can still hear within:
Tick-tock, tick-tock, tick-tock.

* * * * *

Confined to her cell, Marie Antoinette passed the long days by reading, sewing and knitting. On one occasion the jailer's wife brought her youngest child, a boy of eight years, to see the Queen, hoping it would lift her spirits. Marie Antoinette took the boy in her arms and lavished affection on him as she tearfully commented on her own son, who was the same age and whose miniature portrait and curl of hair she kept on her person. Her emotional outburst touched the hearts of her jailers, who thereafter, and sometimes at great risk to themselves, brought visitors into the prison to see her. One of those who came was the Abbé Magnin, who heard her confession and gave her Communion.

An attempt to rescue her was planned for 2 September 1793, but again the plot unravelled at the crucial moment and some of those involved, including the jailer and guards, were themselves imprisoned.

After this unsuccessful escape attempt, Marie Antoinette was moved to an even more secure cell. Her only source of daylight now was from a half-bricked-up window, whose upper half was fortified by iron bars. She was refused candles to illuminate the dark evenings and her food was reduced to a minimum. As October approached the days grew shorter, and the nights became colder and the damp more noticeable. Rosalie, the young domestic, did everything in her power to make life as comfortable as possible for the gentle Widow Capet. The lack of exercise and fresh air, coupled with the cold and damp, had an increasingly adverse effect on her health and she suffered bouts of internal bleeding.

During the long nights she prayed at length for her children and friends, and even for her enemies. Sometimes she would reminisce on her past life. She thought of the man who secretly loved her – the Swede, Count Fersen – knowing that his love would never be fulfilled. She remembered the times he made his feelings known in subtle ways as she addressed him in thought:

FERSEN

Greetings, dear Fersen,
Noble count of envied looks and charm,
Romantic cavalier of wars and masquerades thru' the years.
Your eyes betrayed the love you felt for me,

Knowing that I was beyond your reach
And yet your prudent nature stifled all alarm
And put at ease my naked fears.
Where now, brave Fersen, do you wander,
With my image embodied in your heart?
A battlefield afar – I pray not –
Where glory falsely parades and bathes itself in blood?
How could such cruelty be looked upon as art?
But you, gentle Fersen, could not be a willing messenger of
death.
Your noble nature could not harbour within its delicate
construction,
Such a divisive threat,
Without betraying itself even in unrequited love –
That same love that recites its happy song
In my fond memories of you,
The brief encounters, the warm greetings,
The intriguing guesses of masquerades
And the endearing echoes of happy hours
That linger still in nostalgic meetings,
As I reminisce and now begin to visualise,
Beyond my prison bars,
The soft tread of autumn,
As it caresses the drowsy trees
And indulges its ancient art,
Unconcerned by the malevolent influence of impetuous Mars.
Alas, dear Fersen!
Destiny has decreed that we shall not meet again in this earthly
existence.
Unaware, I have by naive word and deed,
My ill-timed appointment with death secured.
And now I wait with cold anticipation the final journey to that
infamous arena,
Without resistance,
Where, by ambitious guile and dark intrigue,

The unsuspecting are daily lured.
Alas, dear Fersen!
Saying goodbye is always sad,
But, for ever, it is the death of hope.
Farewell, dear friend.

* * * * *

As September drew to a close, Marie Antoinette's thoughts dwelt on autumn with its vivid, changing colours, mature fruit and nostalgic odours. Whilst knitting or reading she would mentally wander back in time to Versailles Palace and her Petit Trianon that she loved so much, to relive the happy periods. This was now her only comfort. She longed to be free to wander at will through the colourful autumn scenery. She breathed deep the fragrant atmosphere whilst mentally tracing the mingling odours to their source. Although cruelly denied even a sight of the outside world, her imagination flourished. She sat in her chair, her fair hair turned completely grey by her ordeal, and her blue eyes, which seemed to illuminate her aged face, stared intently at the light from the barred upper half of the window. She imagined the painted landscape of the outside world and silently praised autumn's artistic splendour:

AUTUMN

Greetings, bountiful autumn,
Majestically portrayed in vibrant, colourful dress,
And extravagantly endowed with life's necessities untold,
Artistically inspiring the pregnant earth that you lovingly
    caress
And whose prodigious effort is by me and all the world extolled.

Times often I felt your lingering presence by laden trees,
That extended far in wide expanse,
And whose richly painted fruits you plumped with ease,
Whilst impregnating them with haunting varieties of taste and divine
*   fragrance,*
And on whose identifying leaves you breathed warm shades of
*   yellow, orange and red,*
To complement the shades of green in dappled intrusion,
To lavishly impress and fill with joy the admiring eyes they fed
And the fauna of the wild was equally embraced without exclusion.

O, what joy to wander free out there again, amid your colourful
*   extravagance!*
And to mingle with the happy toilers in the fields, gathering the
*   harvest,*
And there to spill my honest sweat and in humility advance
And feel the flush of contentment on being so blest,
And there to sit with friends at day's end and sing the songs of old,
And watch the silhouettes of happy-sounding,
*   homeward-winging rooks, west,*
In long extended queues across an embered sky of fiery gold
And there to feel at one with God, and in His presence rest.
But alas! I can only dream of happy autumn days, my unforgotten
*   own,*
That spill from nostalgic memories, gently cascading from the past,
As I languish in this cold, damp, lonely prison cell alone.
Once a fragrant rose in royal pose, whose petals now alas! are fading
*   fast.*
O, let me sleep for evermore in your all-endearing bosom, lovely
*   autumn,*
When the die is finally cast and I too am just a memory of the
*   past.*

* * * * *

In that same colourful outside world of autumn the struggle for power and change continued unrelentingly. Men and women – priests and nuns included – were being daily guillotined. Any belief or principle that seemed a threat or hindrance to the revolutionary ideal was brutally suppressed. The policies of the Ancien Régime, if not already dead, were certainly bleeding to death. Marie Antoinette's enemies were pressing hard now for her trial, and their pressure was soon rewarded by the announcement that it was to begin at eight o'clock on the morning of 14 October 1793.

The trial continued for two full days and nights, but the guilty verdict had been decided beforehand. All the charges against her were the evil inventions of corrupt minds. Nothing could be proved against her, but her vile accusers were undeterred in the pursuit of their goal. She answered all their accusations in a calm and dignified manner, but at four o'clock on the morning of 16 October 1793, the guilty verdict was announced. The sentence of death was passed, to be carried out at noon the same day. Marie Antoinette kept her self-control and calmly accepted her fate.

She was then escorted back to the Conciergerie and placed in the condemned cell. She sat and wrote her last letter to her beloved children and Madame Elizabeth, into whose care she entrusted her loved ones. The tear-stained letter was confiscated by an official and never delivered. She then lay on her bed, exhausted and weeping, facing a small window through which the early morning light filtered. As she wept she invoked the spirit of her dead mother, the former Empress of Austria, Maria Theresa:

INVOCATION

O, my dear departed mother,
Had I but lingered on your illuminating and bridled my
*   impetuosity,*
My untimely end would not now be measured in hours –
Hours whose hungry seconds tirelessly devour time
And draw me ever closer to this final atrocity.
The cold, insensitive blade stands poised in idle wait,
Ready to perform its dreadful deed,
Stilling the breath of life in a momentary, violent rush,
As would a lowly hoe a troublesome weed.
O, dear departed mother, and all those heaven-haunting angels
*   and saints*
In whose pious company you now dwell,
Intercede for me and ask almighty God to grant me the spiritual
*   strength,*
My besieging fear to quell,
And face my end with dignity,
As I kneel beneath the guillotine
And whisper my forgiveness to France.
Amen.

* * * * *

Marie Antoinette was still lying down when Rosalie arrived to assist her in changing her clothes. Tears had formed rivulets down the deposed Queen's troubled face and dampened the clothing around her neck. Rosalie's tears mingled with the Queen's. The change of clothes, even now, had to be carried out in the presence of a watchful guard.

How long the condemned Queen of France would have survived the living conditions she was subjected to, had she been allowed to live on, is a matter of conjecture. Her health had certainly deteriorated, both physically and mentally, which was exactly as her enemies had hoped.

Rosalie tried to comfort her whilst she herself was distraught with grief. Having completed her duties, the young domestic departed in tears, unable to bring herself to say farewell for fear of causing more upset to the condemned Queen and herself.

Alone again, Marie Antoinette lay on her bed and, seemingly oblivious of her surroundings, allowed her thoughts to drift back in time to the place where her happiest days were spent – the Petit Trianon, which her husband, the King, had presented to her as a marriage gift, together with a symbolic, jewel-encrusted key. She relived some of those happy memories of that one place where her spirit would always live on:

THE PETIT TRIANON

Pretty Petit Trianon,
My haven of joy,
Where contentment oozed from every thought
And no whisperings of sadness ever seemed to wander by.
Times often among your cultured rooms in thought I strayed,
As inspiration soared to dizzy heights,
Revealing all its secret art to me in imagery displayed,
As I lay in bed awake, content,
In the serene solitude of warm summer nights,
Whilst the cricket and the corncrake piped aloud,
From near and far their ancient calls,
Mingling with the soothing fragrance of roses,
Wafting on the wings of air,

From their beds beneath your ivied walls.
But there in spirit shall I ever dwell,
To wander endlessly unseen
Among your gay, contented rooms with happy song,
To fill my days and nights
And never have to be again a queen.
Farewell, my haven of joy –
But only for a little while –
My lovely Petit Trianon.

* * * * *

As the appointed hour drew near she was roused from her daydreaming by the sudden echo of drumbeats, and immediately her thoughts were on the guillotine and the sombre crowd that would be gathered around it to witness her sad exit from life. Again she stared at the illuminated window and mentally resigned herself to her fate:

RESIGNATION

The drums of death sound their fearful notes,
That marshal me to where I die.
And there, amid the confusion of violent change,
I must embrace death
And give to my insidious enemies
Their moment of rootless joy,
There beneath the awesome guillotine,
Where the angel of death stands unseen in patient stay,
Ready to release the blemished soul at life's end,
And guide it to its judgement fate –
To Heaven I hope, thru' Purgatory perhaps,
But not to Hell, I pray.
Amen.

* * * * *

Shortly before her departure from the Conciergerie, several tribunal officials arrived in her cell and, following the rule of law, again read aloud the death sentence to her. A few minutes after they left, her executioner, Henri Sanson, the son of her late husband's executioner, entered her cell. He introduced himself and then, in a solemn and businesslike manner, he instructed her to join her hands behind her back, where he bound them tightly together. He then removed her bonnet, cut her hair short around her neck and replaced the bonnet. Then he led her, by a trailing rope tied around her waist, out of the Conciergerie to a waiting tumbril, yoked to a pair of workhorses.

The King had been escorted to his execution the previous January in a manner befitting his royal status – in a royal carriage – and he had been proved guilty of the charge of high treason; Marie Antoinette was guiltless, but she had become the revolution's convenient scapegoat – an innocent victim. So they found it expedient to sacrifice her. The tumbril was the final humiliation, but she accepted it uncomplainingly. She climbed, unassisted, on to the lowly horse cart, where she was made to sit facing backwards next to a revolutionary priest. The priest had been provided by her enemies as a mocking gesture, and she ignored him during the whole of their forty-five-minute journey through the streets of Paris. Sanson held the trailing rope attached to her waist as he guided the horses to their destination in the Place de la Revolution under heavy escort. As the cart pulled away from the Conciergerie, Marie Antoinette turned to look at the building and mentally bade it goodbye:

RELIEVED

Goodbye, oppressive Conciergerie,
My dark cell of sorrow,
Where anguish and pain filled my depressed days and sleepless
*   nights.*
I rejoice that there is no tomorrow
To be subdued by your depressing sights.
Free of your stifling grasp,
I now begin by tumbril and with fettered hands
The final journey unafraid.
Condemned I am and soon to die,
And therewith my existence deleted,
But my innocence thru' time unblemished stands.
Goodbye for ever, dark Conciergerie.
Goodbye.

* * * * *

The route to the Place de la Revolution was double-lined with revolutionary soldiers. Fears of an attempted rescue somewhere along the route were strong. The crowds, almost silent, lined the streets behind the soldiers to gaze compassionately at the calm and dignified woman who was their queen. She sat in pensive mood, showing no sign of fear, having already resigned herself to her fate.

As the tumbril entered the Place de la Revolution she caught sight of the Tuileries Palace, on whose balcony she had stood over twenty years before to be enthusiastically welcomed by the crowds in that same square. She felt an emotional surge as she thought of it and the dreams she had had on that day, but she had had to say goodbye to those dreams. She cried within as she silently and emotionally framed her last farewell:

BELOVED FRANCE

Farewell, my beloved France.
You loved me in my youth, when song and sanity prevailed
And the lily bloomed supreme.
I loved you too;
And even now, within my broken heart,
The embers of the fire that burned
Still warmly glow serene –
But not, alas, for long!
The guillotine stands in sombre mood,
Ready to execute its appalling deed
And destroy for ever the remnants of my dream.
I forgive you, France,
And pray that you forgive me too,
As you stand in queue, a multitude to witness my demise.
The rose of Versailles, a faded flower,
Never again shall see the morning sunrise.
And as I embrace death on this beautiful autumn day,
I pray that Heaven will welcome my soul back home again
    without delay.
Farewell, my beloved France.
Farewell for ever.
Amen.

* * * * *

The tumbril came to a halt and she climbed down unaided. Without hesitation she climbed the steps on to the scaffold, where she shook the bonnet from her head and calmly waited for the preparations to be concluded. When her head was in position beneath the weighted blade, she whispered her final prayer:

FORGIVE

Almighty God,
I beg again forgiveness for my sins
And for the sins of those
Who by wicked words and deeds
My untimely exit from life
This moment now devised.
Forgi —

BEYOND THE PALE OF LIFE

Thru' the flower-filled fields and byways of Heaven,
She now freely wanders with saintly souls in ethereal dress unseen.
And the sublime fragrance of contentment oozes from every particle
of her spiritual presence,
Free from the ambitious greed and tyranny of wayward men
And free from the constraints, pretences and formalities of an earthly
queen.
In the Petit Trianon one might sense her presence in passing,
And by the lakeside of her hamlet retreat.
Is that her in spiritual dance rippling the waters' brow?
And what is that caressing, musical hum that soothes the mind?
Is it her sweet lullaby of contentment that forms the light wind's
sough?
Unrestrained, her spirit wanders the Versailles domain
And lingers in favourite haunts, where devotees evoke memories of
the past.
Inspired by her spiritual presence, they excel in thought.
Her spiritual essence,
There and in the minds of those who applaud her innocent character,
Will thru' centuries last.